Make Your Own Book Cover

and

Some Book Making Tips

For Paperback and Digital Books

Make Your Own Book Cover
And
Some Book Making Tips
For Paperback and Digital Books
Copyright © 2017 I. R. Awake

~

Published in the USA

~

Introduction

Making a book cover from scratch is not as hard as you think it is. These pages will take your fears away.

Many authors think that making a book cover can be way too much work for them to do, or they think they can never learn all that is needed to do one. That is because they don't know a few tricks and shortcuts. Just follow along and this book will have you making a quality book cover from scratch in a very short time. Samples are shown to help with explanations.

You will also find some helpful bits of information concerning what you need to know for your manuscript.

~

This book was written in a manner to avoid a lot of excess words and it will take you straight to the points of what you need to know to get a quality book cover made EASILY. This is not one of those books where it takes ten pages, to fill up space, to tell you what could be said on one page or less.

The choice was made to publish the pages in COLOR to make points and samples clear for you. Unfortunately color printing is more expensive.

~

Free programs for use are shown in this book. The author has no connection to them other than the author uses them and they were used to make this book.

~

INDEX

Chapter 1 – Your Text Pages

To start, you need to know the size of your book. Most paperbacks tend to be 6' x 9' but you can change it to suit yourself. Set the size of your book (your manuscript) BEFORE you start typing.

The size of manuscript that you choose for a paperback can be used for a digital book.

The cover that you use for your paperback can also be used for your digital book and actually should be used so the two book covers match perfectly.

A Few Things That Often Confuse People

Most people write their manuscript in the program Word which saves in the form of .doc for document. To upload your manuscript for a **paperback**, you need to save that Word.doc in the form of a PDF and then upload that PDF. In the program Word, see the arrow for choices of format to save in and you will see the PDF option. Save your Word.doc also as a doc file in case you want to make changes.

To upload your manuscript for a digital book (like a Kindle book), you need to upload a Word.doc. Save a copy of your Word.doc as one will be your original formatted for a paperback book and the second will be reformatted for a digital book. Name each accordingly.

A paperback book: What you upload in the form of a PDF is what you will get.

A digital book: These are flowable books. They have no page numbers. You need to remove page numbers from your digital manuscript (your second copy of the Word.doc) if you had entered them.

A digital book does not act or look as if it is a regular book. You should have breaks between the chapters.

With both types of books, you do need to 'justify' the lines. Note as you are reading here that words begin and end evenly on all lines. That is done up at the top area of your Word.doc where you should see four areas of horizontal lines. You want all lines to use the far right choice unless you want to center wording or to center a photograph.

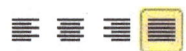

When you are trying to center wording or a photograph, make sure that in the Word program paragraph area that there is no number in the area that says 'By:' as follows in the area for Indentation. If you have a number in that area, your view will not be perfectly centered. Depending on the year of your program, it may be found under a tiny arrow to the right of the word 'Paragraph'.

Some people prefer to do a digital book first while others prefer to do the paperback first. It is your choice and you may decide not to do a paperback.

A paperback book has mirrored pages to allow for a book spine. A digital book does not have this.

When you want to add a view into your Word.doc, use the INSERT tab. Do NOT copy and paste something into your Word.doc.

~

At times a person may have a problem with something connected to formatting not being right. They cannot get it to change.

Some people work in HTML and use two or three programs to bring their book together. If you want to be that 'busy', this book is not for you.

Three tips if you are having a problem

1 – Make sure the paragraph indent is set correctly. See sample view above.

2 – Make sure you have the line spacing as 'Don't add space between paragraphs of the same style' unless for some reason you do want a space between EVERY line.

3 – At times you may not know why words are not doing what you want them to. You can check on the backward looking 'P' (¶) above under the Home tab by the Paragraph settings and it will show formatting. Many don't understand the meanings so, put your mouse curser at the end of the best area. Click on delete – delete – delete until the bad area comes up to it and disappears. Then redo the area that was a problem.

~

Adding Page Numbers

Both a paperback and a digital book have a way to find things. However, the paperback has page numbers and the digital book has links. Adding both automatically is found under the INSERT tab and then Page Number. You may have to make your view wide to see it.

The paperback pages are numbered on the bottom of the page and they mirror each other. (The left page has the number on the left. The right page has the number on the right.)

~

Adding an Index or Table of Contents

This may vary a little per the edition of your Word program.

If you wrote your book in the program Word, you need to do the following:

(1) Type in the word 'Contents' or 'Index' where you are going to want your index.
(2) Highlight the area for each chapter (on the words) and make sure you have chosen the index with NO page numbers for a digital book (as they do not show page numbers) or WITH page numbers for a paperback. Click on 'Heading 1' under Styles for each chapter title.
(3) Put your mouse on the page where you want your table of contents to begin. Under the 'Reference' tab, click on 'Insert Index'.
(4) When done, highlight the word you typed (Contents or Index) and go to the 'Insert' tab. Click on 'Bookmark'. In the area that opens, type in, using **small** letters, toc and then click on add.

Test it out on a few random Word.doc's until you understand the concept.

~ ~ ~

Chapter 2 – Your Book Theme

I am going to assume you do have your book written and that you are to the point where you need to put a cover on it. You have probably thought about what you want the cover to look like, but don't be surprised if you change that idea as you actually work on the cover.

Your goal is to have a cover that is an instant draw for a sale. You must gain the attention for a possible buyer within the first second the potential buyer glances at the cover. It must look attractive, balanced and interesting, plus make the person want to see what is inside the book.

You have probably seen books where you know the book cover has been hand drawn by a non-artist and wonder why the author didn't put a better front cover on the book. If that is you, you do need this book.

To give you an example of the focal point on a cover from bad to better, but not great, following are two samples for a western theme book. Viewing these two should easily make my point. The first is hand drawn out of desperation. The second is an actual photograph. The color view will definitely grab more attention than the hand drawn one.

To take a view to another stage and adding wording, following is a third sample. Notice the brightness in comparison to the first two views. The photograph below is actually only about one-half of the original, omitting a lot of background, and the sky area has been tripled.

Chapter 3 – Samples

Before getting to the section of how to do a cover, it is important that you understand what you can do. Often a person is totally confused so hopefully this chapter will help. Play around with the FREE on line program noted further in this book as you can always change things and delete things out. These few samples explain how things were done.

Sample One

The finished sample previously shown shows how the right decision for a view can bring a title together.

The view (JPEG) was cropped, leaving out much on the sides. A thin blue sky was copied and stretched, then added to make the sky area larger.

- The main title was a premade store logo sign and the text type, the text, size and color was changed.
- The word 'and' was a separate text entry with a different text type and size chosen.
- The words 'His Dog' was a third text entry with the size and text type chosen for it.

Sample Two

'Mamma Said' was done in fast stages. The author wanted a very plain and yet elegant look.

First a dark background was added filling the full book cover. Two separate lines would have also worked.

Second, the main focal item and its background had the color changed which gave it the light brown background. That was added and stretched to almost the top and bottom of the background giving it a line at the top and bottom.

Third, the title and author name was added using different text types and sizes.

Sample Three

The background is a crop from a photo that was enlarged.

The girl is a crop from a second photo. It then had all background removed and was made transparent. The girl was added on top of the background and then she was sized.

The author name and title areas were preset text forms. The words were then changed.

Sample Four

The view is one photograph. Nothing except the metadata being removed was done to the view. It is actually only part of a full view.

To it was added only the two text areas from preset word forms.

The wording and the word colors were changed.

Sample Five

The portrait view was sized to fit the width of the front book cover. The coloring around Alexander is original to the 1861 portrait.

A section of the background was cropped and enlarged to fit at the top and bottom. The resize of that piece came out lighter than the original. It was kept as an accent and then wording was added.

Chapter 4 – Uploading

This chapter will tell you how to upload your own book covers at Amazon CreatSpace website so you understand where you will be headed for a **paperback** book. Other book sites vary with operations.

This chapter does not apply for a digital book, as like a Kindle book. There you upload the front cover and have no template to work with.

If you have been trying to upload a book, you may have discovered that at Amazon for the Kindle area, they now offer to upload a paperback. A word from those who know: Don't upload a paperback there. There have been many problems and currently, as this book is being written, it is in the beta stage. It also appears that the covers done there can instantly be spotted with the look they have. Currently and luckily, they can be deleted because other benefits are available through CreateSpace.

Upload your paperback at CreateSpace.com, which is part of Amazon, for your own sanity. They currently offer two formats that allow you to upload your own book covers as well as preset designs where you can do alterations. You can choose a matte or glossy book cover finish.

~

To upload your finished book covers at CreatSpace, you have two choices. Both are on page four of your template choices.

The Palm. Size is 6' x 9' and it says Spineless. This HOWEVER does allow you to use their color index to put a solid color spine on your book and text on the spine of your own color choice. Follow the prompts and just chose the color you want and it is there. This template is what you will use. Note that you do need at least 131 pages to put <u>text</u> on a spine.

The Pine. Size is 6' x 9' and it says Spineless. You WILL have to have your spine built into a solid front and back cover, sized for your page thickness to use this. Until you are proficient in understanding how to do your own spine, the thickness needed, and adding both the front and back as one JPEG, stay away from this.

Concentrating on The Palm, you will upload your front cover and then your back cover. You will choose your spine color, your spine text and text color. Just follow the prompts. If you want to change something, go back and change it while you are on the page. There are times when you may go back and forth a dozen times deciding on the spine color. You can change this later, even after published. Be sure to click on publish when making a change after you have already published the book.

As you work through your options, you will eventually see the full book cover surrounded by a red area. At this time you may want to do a screen capture with a snipping tool of the full view and save it for reference.

Note the red/pink lines along the edges on screen. Anything that you **DO** want to show on your cover should not be in the red/pink trim line. If it is, go back and adjust your cover.

Following is a full view showing the sample of *A Cowboy and His Dog* book cover after choices are made. You will be shown another final copy giving your final results. The blurb and Logo or Photo area will be filled in prior to uploading the covers (see further in this book).

As the book completes, the system will add a barcode for you. This sample reflects a book of 500 total pages so it has a wide spine. In this sample, the system will add the Barcode generated by Amazon.

The red areas will not show on the final product.

Chapter 5 – How to Do It

The routine is pretty much (a) upload one or a few views. (b) Drag and arrange things how you want them, (3) and add text.

STEP 1 – If you have not yet started a computer folder for your book, do so now. Put your manuscript into it. In that folder, start a second folder titled Views. This will hold all JPEG items that you may want to use or need to use for your book cover.

STEP 2 – You are going to need a main view for your book cover. There are many varied photo sites on the web. Some offer free views and allow commercial use, but read all the small print with any view you chose. Two sites to check are Pixabay.com and Canava.com for free photographs. Canava is where the cover magic happens. Any photos you want to save for possible use, download them and save to the 'Views' folder. Save each as a JPEG if it is in another format. Remove any metadata from each view.

The program FastStone Image Viewer (FREE) will do this under the Tools tab.

STEP 3 – At Canava.com, begin with the FREE version until you know what you are doing. You can join the paid version at any time, if needed, and depending on what you may want to do in the future.

Play around for a while so you get used to the program. Anything you do can be changed or deleted.

a. 'Create a Design'. Click on the upper left green tab.
b. Scroll down to 'Blogging and Books'.
c. Choose and click on 'Kindle Cover'. You will use this for paperback and digital books.
d. Check out all the areas on the left.
   - Layouts you will not yet be using while you are learning. They are somewhat restrictive but one may work for you.
   - Elements contain FREE and paid for photos.
   - Text: You will be using the top area for HEADING, SUBHEADING, and TEXT.
   - Background: You will not be using this now.
   - Uploads: This is where you will upload views you have saved for possible use. Upload only what you will use now. To delete a view you upload, click on the 'I' for 'trash' when you hover on a view.
   - TRANSPARENT VIEW: To make a view transparent (eliminate the background). Also see https://burner.bonanza.com/ FREE.

STEP 4 – Choose your main photo for your cover. Make sure metadata is removed. Decide if you want to use the full photo or part of it. Crop to what you want to use and save it changing the name somewhat. Resize the photo to what size you think you will need. Note that a tiny part saved from a full photo will be blurred for full book cover use.

STEP 5 – Upload the view to Canva. It will take a few seconds to upload. Drag it to the cover area. You will see four corners. Drag and expand until the area you want to use it in or the full page template is filled. Note that at times an inner window will show. Click on the X on the upper left that will pop up.

If you want to add more sky or a lower area (expand that area), go to the view in your computer. Crop the area you want. Resize, upload to Canva, and drag to the book area. Expand and adjust as needed.

If you want to add a second or more view, do so.

STEP 6 – Add your TITLE, SUBTITLE, AUTHOR NAME and maybe a short blurb line to the Front Cover. You can move it, size it, and change the color of any text.

To make words different sizes, use a separate 'add' and move it around to where you want it.

STEP 7 –You DO want your view and text to be slightly left of center for a paperback front cover.

STEP 8 – If you are not doing a back cover (you are doing a digital book) you are ready to download it. If you are doing a back cover (page 2), don't download until the back is done. Your covers will auto save in Canva and you can go back later and make changes for a new download.

Download as a JPEG (not a PNG as recommended). Save into a new folder in your book folder titled Book Cover. The procedure for you may be to open the file downloaded, cut and then paste it to that folder. Possibly rename the front as 1 and the back as 2. Those are what you will upload to CreateSpace.

Back Cover

If you are doing a paperback book, you will want a back cover (page 2 at Canva). You can choose a duplicate of your front JPEG, a solid color or chose one of the background choices from Canva.

The main body of the back should have a blurb about your book. Chose a normal size text at Canva for making your back cover blurb. Don't put the text clear to the sides of the pages.

The bottom left corner area (up some from the bottom and to the right of the left edge) is where your logo or author photo should go. Add this in Canva. (You upload it to Canva, then drag it to your cover, size it by dragging the corners and drag it to place.)

Keep the bottom right open on the back cover page for CreateSpace to add a barcode. The system will self-assign one.

Chapter 6 – FREE Programs and Links

Faststone Image Viewer - FREE http://www.faststone.org/
A powerful program that will do many things. You will mainly use this to <u>crop, resize and remove metadata</u>. Be sure to do a save after alterations to a photograph or view. You will have to download this to your computer so make sure you do not have a program that will do all three things noted. You will see other FREE programs at the above link that may be of interest to you.

Background Burner – FREE https://burner.bonanza.com/
This program will remove the background from photos. It can make your photos have a white background or have a transparent background. They offer a paid version.

Canava – FREE www.canva.com This is where you will build your book covers. This is an on-line program, not download program.

There are options for a paid version but play around with this for a while before you make that decision. You may not need the paid version. You can get very detailed with your finished product using this site. The paid version also offers transparent backgrounds for photos.

The above information is current as of this book publication.

Chapter 7 - Photographs FREE and Paid

You will find sites that do offer free photographs. Be sure, if you chose a photo, that the photographer and the site allow free use, specifically COMMERCIAL use for a book. Paid for photographs can have their own rules so always read the terms.

Photographs taken by the U.S. government are usually free of copyright.

There are many places to search, including the Library of Congress (www.loc.gov). Each photo will state its own allowable or known rights of use or rights advisory. Most will say 'No known restrictions'.

It is said that anything written or photographs taken prior to 1923 are copyright free. This is not always so. Use caution.

One site that has free and $1 photos plus other options is www.pixabay.com A web search will bring up current other sites.

Chapter 8 – In Closing

The hardest part of making your own book cover is figuring out what you want to go on it. It is a good idea to search out at least a few things so you can see them side by side in your computer to make a choice between them. Very often what you start out thinking you want will change.

Take a day and play around in the Canva program so you can test all of the varied things you can do for your book cover.

Above all, Have Fun !